Grandpa's house

Written by Robyn Clyne • Illustrated by Katie Keller

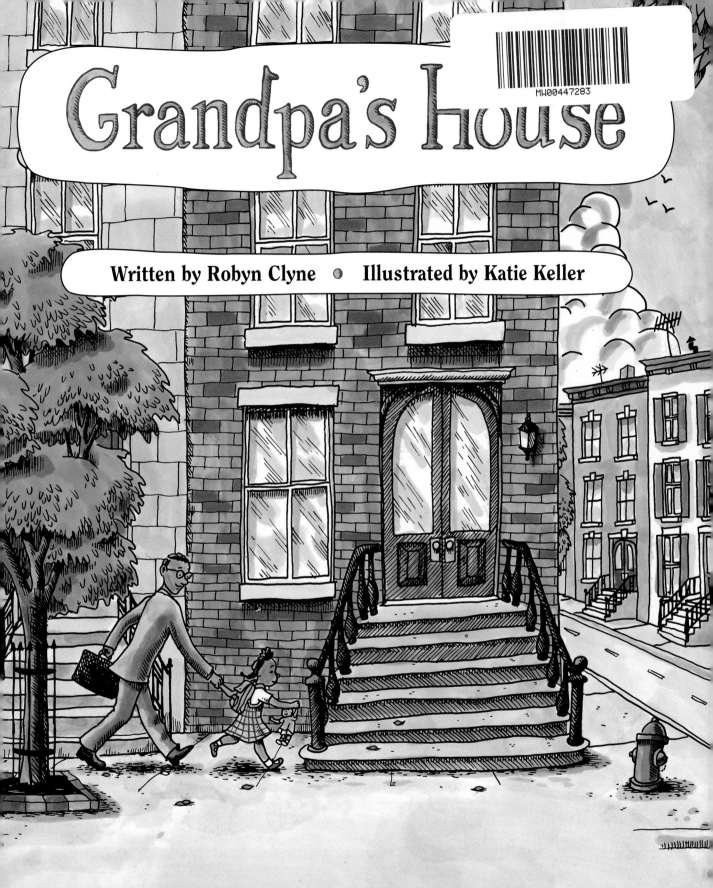

MODERN CURRICULUM PRESS

Program Consultants

Becky Dugan, *Teacher*
Brady Elementary School
Little Rock, Arkansas

Judy Stobbe, *Bilingual Teacher*
Alianza School
Watsonville, California

Debra List, *Teacher*
Hansberry Child-Parent Center
Chicago, Illinois

Wanda Tansil, *Teacher*
University Terrace School
Baton Rouge, Louisiana

Executive Editor: Dorrie Berkowitz

Associate Editor: Marcia Formichelli

Design concept: Lillie Caporlingua/BILL
SMITH STUDIO

MODERN CURRICULUM PRESS
An imprint of Paramount Supplemental
  Education
250 James Street
Morristown, New Jersey 07960

ISBN: 0-8136-7931-1 (single copy)
0-8136-8499-4 (6-pack)

2 3 4 5 6 7 8 9 DP 99 98 97 96 95

Grandpa's house is like a big toy chest,

3

4

full of the things that I like best!

a frisky puppy

6.

a sleepy kitten

a big piano

a nice, warm bed

a tall, brown clock

a story book

and most of all, as you can see,

a rocking chair for Grandpa and me.